earthly

Books by Michael McFee:

Poetry:

Colander
To See (with photographer Elizabeth Matheson)
Sad Girl Sitting on a Running Board
Vanishing Acts
Plain Air

Anthologies:

*This is Where We Live: Short Stories by 25
    Contemporary North Carolina Poets*
*The Language They Speak Is Things to Eat: Poems
    by Fifteen Contemporary North Carolina
    Writers*

earthly

poems by michael mcfee

carnegie mellon university press
pittsburgh 2001

acknowledgments

Thanks to the magazines in which the following poems first appeared:

"The Drowned Pool" in *Blue Moon Review*; "Static," "This Page" in *Carolina Quarterly*; "To Work," "Treadmill," "& Vicinity" in *Five Points*; "Memoir," "Yule Log," "After Song," "Glory" in *Hudson Review*; "Vita Brevis," "Goodyear" in *Kenyon Review*; "To My Father on the Anniversary of His Death" in *The New Republic*; "Smoking Cigarettes on the Fire Escape" in *The News & Observer*; "Afterlives" in *Now & Then*; "The Angel" in *North Carolina Literary Review*; "The Four Seasons" in *Ontario Review*; "Poem Typed on an Old Machine with a Bi-Chrome Ribbon," "Bruises" in *Poetry*; "Phantoum" in *Prairie Schooner*; "Those Words" in *Shenandoah*; "Wait," "Four-Leaf Clover," "The Whistler," "Ella Fitzgerald" in *Southern Review*; "Openings," "Earthly," "Twitch," "The Family Laugh" in *Tar River Poetry*; "Woman in a Second-Story Corner Room," "Nothing," "Honeysuckle" in *TriQuarterly*.

"Poetry Reading in a Room Hung with Bayard Wootten Photographs from Depression-Era North and South Carolina" was issued as Second Sunday Broadside #1 by the North Caroliniana Society, University of North Carolina at Chapel Hill.

Thanks also to the Institute for the Arts and Humanities and the College of Arts and Sciences, UNC-Chapel Hill, for providing leave time to work on this book. And thanks, as always, to Michael Chitwood and Alan Shapiro, for helpful comments and generous support.

The publication of this book is supported by a grant from the Pennsylvania Council on the Arts.

Book design by Lisa Ferrugia.

contents

o n e

t w o

t h r e e

four

five

six

for robert morgan

one

to work

Brookshire had come to work second shift
at Walker Manufacturing the day it opened

and stayed until the recession shut it down
a dozen years later. He was an end finisher,

six-foot-four and strong enough to hang
the bent and welded tailpipes and mufflers

on a fast-moving chain that would loop them
through a room-sized oven for rustproofing.

He loaded and unloaded them left-handed
until that arm was so muscular it looked

like the claw of a human fiddler crab,
until that hand was so thickly calloused

he didn't need to wear protective gloves
when he handled the rough or heated metal.

He liked the work, its good wage and routine
and not having to think about what he did.

He liked his forearm, its Popeye tattoo
that slowly vanished underneath the grime

of a nine-hour shift, as daylight itself
clocked out while he worked. He liked leaving

the plant at one-thirty in the morning
exhausted, especially in the summer,

walking into the cool mountain night
dark as the water that would soon be flowing

from his skin as he carefully scrubbed away
all the filth that had seeped through his clothes,

blackening his pale body utterly
except where his underwear and socks had been.

His sleep was clean and deep and very long.
To work is to get dirty then get paid.

t r e a d m i l l

Somebody has rolled out the black carpet welcoming me to middle age
but it's a tease, this sidewalk spinning backwards, this relentless loop,
I have to pace briskly just to stay in place, staring out the gym window

at the back of the town's post office, the loading dock with its chaos
of trays, boxes, carts, canvas bins, forklift flats, tall metal cabinets,
scraps of paper and tape and stamps underfoot, postal detritus,

the battered tractor-trailer backed into the bay, loaded all night
with its perishable contents and now puffing past the ready platoon
of numbered jeeps and panel vans, headed for a distribution center

in a larger city where letters from this and hundreds of other zip codes
will be directed toward thousands of carriers and millions of addresses
and I wonder if the postcard I just mailed has a prayer of ever arriving

and I know, as the breakneck conveyor belt keeps spinning under me,
that my father would say *Sure it does son* and explain the whole process,
my late father who never exercised once in over 50 working years

and spent 33 of them on the graveyard shift at the post office
because the pay differential was worth it, a dime or so an hour,
he could tell me why what is stacked where, how who will do what when,

he could tell me how lucky it was for a high-school graduate to survive
the depression and the war and (worst of all) the civil service exam
and actually land a job as a postal clerk downtown in his hometown

just as he was getting married and buying a house and starting a family
for whose sake he'd work the odd hours that kept him from seeing them much
except maybe at dinner, when he was still in his bathrobe, just waking up,

he could tell me exactly how that man over there, leaving work, feels
as he walks across the emptied dock every morning at 8:30, stretching,
his shift over at last, blinking into the huge unfluorescent light

and lighting a cigarette for the stroll across the lot to his cold car
and the drive back to bed, to sleep away the day like some kind of bat,
his fingertips filthy from handling letters, inked deep as a criminal's,

smearing his face and steering wheel and stick shift and radio knobs
as he yawns his way home, smoking, Rural Route 2, delivering himself,
the black road turning under his feet as he passes the boxes lifting their flags.

smoking cigarettes
on the fire escape

From this distance,
cigarettes and smoke invisible,
they seem to be speaking

a kind of sign language to each other.
He lifts his open hand to his face
as if to take back a sentence,

then slowly lowers it and tilts his head
back to face the sky.
She does the same,

then extends her arm full-length,
jabbing her finger toward the ground.
What point is she trying to make to him?

They keep exchanging these gestures
until he covers his face one last time
and flicks a word to the landing,

crushing it with his foot.
Again she does the same.
The man reaches for his heart,

then taps his hands together, bearing
something to their waiting lips,
starting the dumb show again.

They're probably just a couple
of bored office workers
turning their morning break into smoke,

but I can't help seeing my parents
years ago, waiting outdoors
for the doctor's news,

sneaking back into their bodies
for one more cigarette,
resuming their unheard conversation.

vita brevis

The old man I could mistake for my father
cruises the grocery lot for the perfect space,
then parks his car and opens its heavy door

and slowly emerges from that private shade
into August's unconditioned heat and light,
blinking and grimacing as he undertakes

his little walk across the shimmering lot:
I watch him falter as the afternoon sun
ripens his naked head before he makes it

under the welcome shadow of that awning
and vanishes behind dark glass, down the aisles
of a store cool and bright as any heaven,

where so much food is stacked so deep and high
he'll never reach it, no matter how hard he tries.

openings

When Dad took his glasses off, which was rarely,
he'd rub his face so hard with both big hands
I thought he wanted to erase his features,
press those weary blue eyes into his head,
flatten that nose and wipe away that grimace
and whisk away the whiskers and new wrinkles

but he never did, he always came back *Dad*:

sometimes I'd watch him nap, his worn glasses
watching us both from the bedside table,
a little *me* bending in his thick lenses
to study those twin deep oval bruises
on either side of the bridge of his nose,
the marks so dark they looked like openings

that he might breathe through in some other life.

e a r t h l y

"I have no *earthly* idea," my mother would say
any time we cornered her with a question
she couldn't or didn't want to answer,
tossing her troubled head back with a laugh
big and yellow as her teeth, turning away
into the refuge of that mortal adjective.

Ten years gone, I wish I could ask her now:
Is there really a heaven where every question
is answered, whether spoken aloud or not?
Or is earth the final idea we're left with,
surrounding our graves like a massive dream
whose gravity we can never quite escape?

"I have no *earthly* idea," my mother would say.

two

y u l e l o g

Just before Christmas, every year,
Dad's rich friend Winston would send one
packed in dry ice, in a special box
stamped *Biltmore Dairy* in dark green cursive.

We'd bear it to the kitchen counter
and juggle the smoking ice into the sink
and slowly unroll the frozen paper
around this first and sweetest of presents:

a yule log made of *Premium* ice cream.
Its chocolate rind looked exactly like bark,
down to the scattered nut-knots;
its pith was a plug of creamy butter pecan

so authentic it almost had rings.
Mom held the long knife under the spigot
until it was finally hot enough
for Dad to slice a piece for each of us,

a thin section from that section
of the tree of endless good cheer and luck
and wealth enjoyed at the Estate.
But we weren't jealous, there in the kitchen

of our home built of skinny logs
on land owned long ago by George Vanderbilt:
as dry-ice fog tried to sneak
cheap melodrama into the scene, we simply

stood on the verge of Christmas
then filled our empty spoons and lifted them
and burned that log in our mouths,
its cold fire falling, filling our aching chests.

the cuban
missile crisis

"All right, class: put your heads down on your desks
and don't look up until I tell you to,"
said Mrs. Moore to her fourth-grade children.
We did as she said because we adored
this stout young teacher, so densely freckled,
who enjoyed recess more than we did,
who'd knock our pitched softballs a country mile
and round the bases announcing, "Home run!"

"O.K., boys and girls: are all heads down?
Good. Listen, children: I want you to pray."
She often had us recite the Lord's Prayer
after the morning Pledge, hands over our hearts,
but we'd never done it this way before.
"I want you to pray two different prayers,"
she whispered. "First, say a prayer to Castro.
Pray for Castro to bring you some candy."

We hesitated, puzzled: pray to *him*?
Hadn't she been telling us how bad he was,
with communist missiles down in Cuba
aimed straight at our defenseless valley school?
"Go ahead, everybody. Pray out loud."
We mumbled something, not sure what to say,
our guided words muffled by folded arms,
then waited a long time, in odd silence.

"All right now, class. You may lift up your heads.
Do you see any candy on your desks?
Did Castro bring you anything to eat?"
"No ma'am," we admitted in unison.
She rubbed her big calloused hands together:
"Please close your eyes and put your heads back down.
And this time I want all of you to pray
to Jesus. Ask Him to bring you candy.

"Pray hard, and keep your heads down, like I said:
and don't look up, until I tell you to!"
We offered our sweet requests to the Lord
and heard a rustling down every aisle
as if some barefoot angel had passed by,
touching our bowed heads and our little desks.
We waited again for Mrs. Moore's voice.
"You may," she said at last, "open your eyes."

And right there, in each shallow pencil tray,
was some hard candy wrapped in cellophane.
Our teacher stood behind her desk, smiling.
"Now, Castro didn't bring you anything,
but Jesus brought you just what you asked for.
Go ahead and eat it, boys and girls."
Mrs. Moore nodded, tickled deeply pink,
as she watched us savoring that manna.

What did we learn, that October morning?
That Castro was a godless dictator?
That Jesus was possibly dangerous,
luring children with pieces of candy?
What could we know of prayer or politics
or anything except we'd pleased the teacher?
No pinpoint freckles could possibly cloud
the joy that flushed her victorious face.

r a m p a n t

Every spring, around May Day,
when Scott Rainwater started to sniff the air,
we knew what was coming:

his Indian blood had begun to stir again
and before long he'd miss several days of school,
climbing into the mountain forest
to gather ramps, the wildest of onions,
which, our teachers warned, looked pretty as lilies
but tasted like the very devil,

if you eat them, children, you'll be sorry,
and so will every other creature unlucky enough
to be anywhere in your vicinity!

That's exactly how everybody knew
when Scott Rainwater had finally come back
after taking his spring tonic:
that smell, intensely foul yet sweet,
pure birth and blossom and raw green urgency,
pouring from all his pores,

his odor so triumphantly repellent
that squeals and nose-held *pee-yous* followed him
as he walked down the hall

rampant with his own ripeness,
fingering the homemade amulet of ramps
strung around his neck,
calmly whistling toward the office
for the principal's annual rite of expulsion,
the longed-for casting-out.

m e m o i r

I don't remember the year, the date, the day
of the week or time of the weekday, the weather
outside the schoolhouse window or inside the room
when I volunteered to read that now-forgotten text.
Was it poetry or prose? It was something nobody
was willing to read aloud to the rest of the class
except me, I'd always been bookish, *teacher's pet*,
my eager hand was probably polishing the air
over my head, the invisible student-halo I wore,

though I can't say for sure. I have no earthly idea
if the teacher picked me because I was her lapdog
and she loved me, or because she was just tired
and didn't want to read it herself, or maybe because
(now that I'm a teacher, yes, I can imagine this)
she wanted to set me up to fail, to teach me
a first lesson in hubris, a word I'd never forget.
I simply don't know. I do know that I stood up
and began reading without the least uncertain pause
from a book I'd never seen before, surrounded
by silence and the sense of being chosen, singular,
a soloist sight-reading to the baffled orchestra,
soon I'd finish and the conductor would applaud
and I'd return to my seat shining with rightness!

But then it happened: an odd word loomed ahead:
its letters were like nothing I'd ever seen before:
I knew I could never say or fake or skip it:
it had to be dealt with, pronto: what should I do?
I've tried for decades to remember what it was—
insidious French phrase? polysyllabic behemoth?
simplest English word gone weird, crumbling
to nonsense the instant my eyesight touched it?—
but I can't bring it back, it's vanished forever.

A shrink, presented with such paltry evidence,
might say I repressed those unutterable syllables
out of fear for their consequences in my writing
or became a writer to discover that lost word,
the source of creation's *Fiat*, or of the creator.
And maybe he'd be right. I really can't say
any more than I can finally speak the word itself
or recover the details of that scene long ago
through some sort of hypnotic suggestion
or invent a memory that never really existed:
what I was wearing, which girl sat closest to me,
whether the feeble lights were buzzing overhead,
the ripe smell of our third-floor room in spring.
But I'll never forget plowing through that word

then halting, knowing I'd said it all wrong,
and hearing the teacher snicker, which released
the pent-up laughter in that illiterate class
and paralyzed me where I stood, suddenly
blushing and needing to pee and wanting to die,
the unspoken words on the page still waiting
for me to take them into my big brain and mouth
and say them so that everyone could forget them,
then and at any oblivious time in the future.

the drowned pool

It was our favorite swimming pool in the county
because we could walk straight into the water,
its sides not the usual vertical drop
but a beachlike slope into a huge chlorinated pond
with a concrete bottom and no slimy stuff,
its wooden diving platform way out in the middle.

One summer I learned to swim there, inside the ropes.
One day I learned to kiss there, behind the concession stand.
One night Bo Gasperson snuck in while drunk
and slipped while running to do a bellyflop
and split his forehead on the edge of the platform
and was dead before his buddies pulled him from the water.

Now it's twenty feet under, at the bottom of Lake Duke,
covered by water used to cool the electric plant.
Now we only swim there in our dreams,
walking downslope into the lake and out to the pool
where we dive all night, in perfect slow motion,
from the platform crowded with the county's drowned kids,

their bodies shining as we practice our intricate dives
inside of and yet into the darkest water,
never quite coming down.

static

It was a shocking winter when the deacons
installed wall-to-wall carpet at First Baptist Church.

Nobody wanted to shake the preacher's hand anymore.
One man refused to be baptized, fearing electrocution.

And all the boys in youth group were ecstatic
with the electrostatic thrill of touching the girls

and being detected, the tiny lightning-and-thunder
sizzle and pop of finger touching skin, the inevitable

squeal that followed, and sometimes the hard slap,
at choir practice, during the sermon, in the closet

in sock feet, sparks pentecosting the darkness
during the ceremonial laying-on of hands.

The boys were scolded and punished and prayed over
but they couldn't stop, they were filled with the spirit,

they were supercharged, they were young Zeuses,
they never believed that the one true God might be

sneaking up behind them on the carpet, scuffling
his holy feet, ready to shock the hell out of everybody.

& vicinity

After Dad died, I found a yellowed stack
of *Asheville & Vicinity* directories
and kept a few, not for the obsolete listings—
including his, 684-6284, I still dial it
in my sleep and hear the beige wall phone
ringing in the middle of the house
(where anybody could eavesdrop every word
of my conversations, no matter how well
I whispered or muttered or covered my mouth)
and see my stiff father rise to answer it,
shouting to compensate for the long distance—

but mostly to remind me of that November
when he decided we needed extra money
to pay for everybody's Christmas gifts
and said he'd found the perfect thing to do:
delivering phone books for Southern Bell.
It sounded easy enough—just driving around,
providing a useful service—until he read,
"No matter how bad the weather may be,
do not leave books in mail- or paper-boxes:
you must attempt to hand-deliver directories
to each customer's door, one book per phone."

I was 13, mortified. What if my rich friends
from school saw us cramming stacks of books
into Dad's crummy Ambassador wagon?
What if they saw us creeping and creaking
along the quiet streets of their neighborhoods,
like hick trick-or-treaters way off schedule?
What if they saw me—head down, arms full—
sprinting across their immaculate front lawns
to ring doorbells, hoping no one would answer
so I could toss directories onto WELCOMEs
and make my nightmare slow-motion getaway?

And what if (worst of all) we had to deliver
books to the house of the girl I then adored?
I knew where she lived, I knew her number,
I can still remember it three decades later,
684-5477, I never actually called her up
though I'd walk the two miles from our house
to the Sinclair station with its greasy booth
and put the dime in the slot and pray
for the strength to get past the black dial tone,
its drone hissing like an electric fence
that protected her voice from my eager ear.

In my heart, I cursed my father's scheme.
I cursed the phone books, those floppy bibles,
their fat old testament of family names
and lurid yellow-pages new testament
of merchants whose gospel we couldn't afford.
I cursed the newsprint stench of the pages
and touristy Mountain Sunset cover picture
and small-print list of *& Vicinity* towns
which was exactly where people like us lived
and where we had to hand out all those directories
by the end of November if we wanted to get paid.

But I got lucky. We only worked after supper,
under cover of twilight, and on weekends
so sunny and mild that nobody stayed home.
We weren't assigned the street where She lived.
On the last footsore Saturday of that month,
we were finishing up at the trailer park
in the woods behind the new high school
when I rang the doorbell on a double-wide
and a familiar-sounding voice announced,
"Just a moment, please!" A woman laughed;
the trailer's warped porch trembled underfoot;

then the local TV weatherman walked into view,
wearing nothing but a pair of boxer shorts.
"Thanks very much!" he cried, shaking my hand
as I gave him the book and lowered my eyes,
studying the clouds of thick black hair
that crossed his chest like a threatening front,
lost in the dark forecast of his body
until the woman called out and he turned away
and I heard my father whistling me to the car
now nearly empty, our work almost done,
dusk humming around me like a receiver off the hook.

three

a f t e r l i v e s

h a n d s

I finger my father's hand, its stumpy thumb truncated during the Depression when he worked for Coca-Cola, driving a delivery truck through Asheville's poorest neighborhood, downshifting to first on the hilly narrow streets so people could steal drinks from the back. That place is gone now, leveled during urban renewal: I can see its ghost out the hospital window, shining like a scar.

I finger his square thumb, its permanent nail no bigger than a paring, a stained sliver of moon in the winter sky. My father stirs in his pharmaceutical sleep.

I move to leave, but he grabs my hand like a newborn: a voracious grip, punctuated by squeezes. Is it just muscle and pulse, the heart's involuntary morse, I feel? Or is it (as I want to believe) intentional, the code he taught me as a kid, the love we could speak to each other anywhere without saying anything, three quick squeezes . . .

p h a n t o m s

I was born upstairs in this hospital, and—after complications—was assigned to an oxygen tent in the hall, my anxious parents peering in, breathing for their only son.

A bracelet of bright plastic about the bone.

My mother died here three years ago this month. My father is dying here now. I will not die here, in godforsaken February, haunted by the phantom pain of family.

dream-poem

I dream my mother visits my father and me
in the house where we always lived. She's dead
but nobody mentions it. She seems very unhappy

and won't stay still, she keeps pacing the rooms.
Soon she leaves, walking across the dusky yard
without looking back. As she slowly drives off,

Dad turns and says, "I just don't understand this."

signs

Cardiac Intensive Care. With the heart, how could it be otherwise?

Waiting Room. I fidget in the relentlessly cheerful waiting room,
waiting again for the appointed hours. All around me, people are
rehearsing their pep talks, their unmonitored hearts pounding against
something thicker than blood.

Immediate Family Only. When someone is dying, all family is immediate.

liberty

How I craved this silver dollar,
the last thing Dad laid on his chester drawers
before bed, the first thing pocketed.

517 combat days, son.

He's handled, palmed, fingered it so long
its circumference is warped, its serration bald,
its features worried away.

I flip his fate in the sterile air.
Tails: the captive eagle looks like a vulture,
its wings an ironic V.

Heads: the goddess is exhausted,
her weak eye weary
of scrutinizing the E in E PLURIBUS UNUM,

her bad ear barely able to hear
(like a heartbeat)
1921.

But even after half a century
of friction, the habitual secret rub for good luck,
one word still crowns her fading head:

LIBERTY.

h o l y ,   h o l y ,   h o l y

Visiting Hours, the only canonical hours we keep here.

My father's body flickers, his parched lips twist with a collage of
language, a faint glossolalia. I swab them with a foam sucker, a cheery
cherry flower dipped in water.

Maybe the monitor is senile, maybe it too has suffered a stroke, maybe it
is an outcast prophet chanting the same phrase over and over again . . .

pete and repeat

My dad would say, "If Pete and Repeat were
sitting on a fence, and Pete fell off, who was left?"

"Repeat," I'd answer.

"All right. If Pete and Repeat were sitting on
a fence, and Pete fell off, who was left?"

"Repeat," I'd say again.

"All right. If Pete and Repeat were sitting on
a fence, and Pete fell off, who was left?"

Suckered into his exasperating game, but
doomed by honesty, good manners, and an angry
queasy fear, I had to repeat, "Repeat."

"All right. If Pete and Repeat were sitting on
a fence, and Pete fell off, who was left?"

And so we'd go, until I covered my ears and
ran from the room.

dream-poem

My mother is waiting on the wide shady porch
of an old house in the country. I can't see her
but I can sense her, the rhythm of her rocker.

I've been driven there in a yellow convertible
with the top down. It's early fall. I'm nervous
because I know she'll smell the beer on my breath.

But the dream ends before I get to the steps.

m i s s i o n s

I watch my father labor to breathe, strapped into his oxygen mask like a pilot setting off on another top-secret mission, Destination: Unknown, pushing the envelope.

s o   m u c h   p a p e r

My father's body has been talking a blue streak. Nobody listens for three quarters of a century, but now they've got him wired like an undercover agent or an astronaut, saving every fascinating whisper from the interior.

So his body is dictating non-stop, an autobiography of astonishing detail, a colossal manuscript-in-progress down at the nurses' station. Wolfe's prodigious ghost drifts in from Riverside Cemetery: he is jealous, he never had this many secretaries, not even on his best night could he fill so much paper with so much ink!

I'd like to read the book of my father's body, but I'm not allowed: it's written in a code I don't understand. But I do know that its last line will be a line, the plain geometry of a to b, the shortest distance between two points but infinite in its density.

i . v . ,   t . v .

They tether my father to I.V.s, lash his bruised arms to the mast, anchor him to intricate machines so that gravity can't swallow him through the valley of the shadow of his bed, so that he won't float to heaven through the pay T.V.'s always-open window.

gravity is a jealous god

The day before my father dies, two attendants transfer him to a stretcher simply by untucking the sheet and lifting him still on it, in a makeshift sling. This is not very difficult to do because, by this time, my father is not very heavy. Gravity has been evaporating him during his month in the hospital. His arms and legs are shocking to touch, all bones and skin; his face is shrunken, his mouth a foul fallen cave.

When the men lower my father, his hospital gown rides up. I happen to be looking where his genitals are, or were: there is little left anymore but a white blur, as if they've been airbrushed away.

Gravity is no respecter of persons. I guess if he had lived longer, it would have kept melting my father away until it reached his heart and its freshly-patched aorta, the last mass of ice to thaw.

beaucatcher

I look out the hospital window at Beaucatcher Mountain. Generations of Asheville lovers used to court there, beaus and their catchers spooning, sparking, necking as the town spread its winking lap of lights below. Then an interstate's open cut bisected the mountain, its passionate slopes blasted to so many stories of air.

I wish my father could see his amputated life made whole again: that missing thumbtip; the leveled hilltop neighborhood; those ghostly turnouts on Beaucatcher where he used to park with my mother; my mother . . .

e x e c u t o r

The sheer business of dying
displaces grief, makes it seem a luxury
for the peripheral or lazy,
for those not dealing

with the funeral home and its upper room
of coffins, with proper flowers,
with the freelance preacher,
with neighbors and their heartfelt food,

with the sealed sentence of will and estate,
with the doleful realtor
measuring the house like an undertaker,
with tortuous claims and benefit . . .

I do, I am, I have, I will.
Grief suppressed may never come at all.

a f t e r i m a g e s

Movies depend on persistence of vision, a *trompe l'oeil* whereby the
retina retains each frame's image just long enough that it overlaps with
the next one, creating the illusion of continuity, kinesis, motion
pictures. So do dreams, splicing together footage from the day's
rushes, from memory, from the uncensored id.

And so do the dead, their afterimages lingering among the living for a
while, in a series of vivid cameo appearances.

d r e a m - p o e m

My mother's words glow through closed curtains,
the sad aftertaste of a dream that left me this:

I will lament the most lamentable use of language
that ever was. I will lament the world.

h i s   s n o r e s

A few weeks after my father dies, I dream I am
driving our old Rambler station wagon around the
neighborhood—the green Ambassador, with straight
shift on the column, the one he taught me to drive in
the school parking lot on Sunday afternoons. It is early
evening, early spring, mild, quiet.

Dad is falling asleep in the backseat. He tries
to stay awake, but, as usual, fails: the narcolepsy plays
him like a lure, his head bobbing backwards, tempting
the great black fish we never see. Soon his mouth sags
open and, with a startling gulp, he starts to snore.

In the dream, I drive around and think:

> *His snores a dark tide*
> *flooding the world.*

I stop in front of a friend's house; he waves
and comes across the yard. "Hi," he says, "How's it
going? How's your dad?" As if on cue, Dad fractures
the dusk with a snore so loud it sounds like the
Rambler has backfired. "Oh!" says my friend, stepping
back in surprise. "*Oh*," I whisper loudly, nodding

toward my dad. "I know he *seems* to be in the backseat, but actually he's dead." And then I say to the evergreens: "If such a thing can be a blessing, then this was."

And my dad snores a hearty *Amen,* and sucks in another lungful of dim air, holding it and considering it and savoring it on his palate, a conoisseur of oxygen, a virtuoso of respiration, the Houdini of sleep, and I sit clutching the cracked wheel, waiting for him to come back as he always had before.

r i t u a l

I haul my father's junk mail
to the burning barrel
one last time,

that miracle of carbon and rust
and mostly air, balanced
on cinderblocks in the sideyard.

I deal the letters
evenly, set three matches
to the pyre of sweepstakes and insurance,

watch the fire catch,
the wavy heat ascending in shadow
like fumes at a pump,

the huge flakes of ash
floating
overhead and downwind through the trees.

I wait for a while,
until the pocked body of the barrel
is cool again, then take from it

what I need:
carbon for grief, rust for rage,
and gallons of airy ash for penitence.

afterlives

Gradually, the afterimages of the dead start to fade, become less
frequent: empty screen, empty page, empty seine of sleep . . .

But my father still gets urgent fat envelopes from *Reader's Digest,*
guaranteed offers from Universal Life, invitations from a Christian
Tour group, to which I finally write: "My father is dead. Do you have
any discount tours of the afterlife?"

his body

I dream I am pacing my father's sold house
one last time, scouting for one more memento. I come
to his chest of drawers, that high altar of secrets,
emptied long ago.
    The top drawer is still empty, except for some
roly-polies. Likewise, the second drawer, which has
even more. The third drawer sticks, and once I get it
open it's completely lined with bugs. I have to jerk the
fourth drawer out: it's half-full of grubs. And once I
manage to crack the bottom drawer, it overflows with

bugs and maggots and worms, all pouring out onto the bedroom floor.

   I have to get a broom! I think. *The new owners—*
   But when I turn, there's my father in the doorway, smiling, silent. And slowly I realize that what had seemed a freckle, or mole, or liver spot, or bruise, or scab, is in fact an insect, one of a calm swarm of bugs, so many that I can never brush them all from his body.

g l o v e s

  I pull on my father's old work gloves
  against the stunted month of his dying,
  his sloughed cells still stuck in the fleece,
  my hands warming as his were chilling
  that last hospital day, so stiff

  they felt like a pair of worn-out gloves
  he'd leave in my grip when he slipped away,
  the ghost of his surrendered gestures,
  a trick handshake, a second skin

  my body would take a lifetime to fill
  until that cold day when the gloves finally fit.

f e b r u a r y

I've come to hate the very sound of this month, this runt of the calendar's litter: feeble, febrile February. *Rue* is at its heart.

And I do rue its coming, every year, my parents vanishing again like vapor off a thawing pond: holy smoke.

It's a cul-de-sac, the dead end of the year: dead presidents, dead saints, dead mother and father: dead year.

dream - poem

My mother's pallbearers stumble toward her grave
with a book the exact same volume as her coffin.
As it passes by, I seem to see my name on it.

I want to say to the dark: *This is just a dream.*

four

woman in a second-story corner room

From the sidewalk, I couldn't tell
if she was dressed, or using a mirror, or alone,

all I could see was her silhouette
combing long black hair, up and over and far down,

her head rolling slightly backwards
with every deliberate pull of hand across scalp,

a dozen strokes, two dozen, three,
like she was considering something, again and again,

she was not my mother in heaven
remembering me, she was not my wife before we met

imagining me or somebody better,
she was simply a backlit shape whose steady motion

was brushing the stubborn tangles
out of night, its long damp strands of darkness

slowly drying in the morning sun
as I kept walking by, my head up and back, tingling.

the four seasons

He started the story in summer
because it was summer, and sultry,
and he was hoping to talk her out
of her clothes then into the meadow
of his bed shining across the room.
She sat wilting in an old armchair.
"Oxford, late summer, '74,"
he said, lowering the blunt needle
onto Vivaldi, *The Four Seasons*,
the perfect antique scratchy soundtrack
to the movie he'd rehearsed for weeks.
"Late afternoon rain at the monks' house
on upper St. Giles. No lawn croquet
for Father James. Everyone napping

except me. It's stuffy, and I'm bored,
so I wander to the library
on the second floor, overlooking
Martyr's Corner in the small graveyard
across the street. Tall skinny casements,
cold rain weeping down the leaded panes,
everything gray and lonely outside"—
he grazed her shoulder as he passed by—
"like here in autumn. I really need
something to pick me up, so I flip
through Brother Arthur's box of records,
looking for rock & roll or some jazz.
But it's all Mahler and opera
except for this exact same album,

Le quattro stagioni." He dropped
its mournful cover onto her lap,
letting his new Italian quiver
in the humid air. "I put it on,
and *Winter* flurries through the speakers,
and a woman in a black raincoat
comes walking up St. Giles from downtown,
her step allegro but then slowing
as she nears the cemetery gate
and goes inside, kneeling at one grave
to kiss the headstone with her fingers,
long red hair falling out of her hood
like fire from heaven to warm the dead."
He touched her hair. "We all stayed that way

for what seemed hours—the woman, the rain,
me at the window, watching, waiting—
and then everything unfroze: she rose
and strode off; the sun came out in time
to set; *Spring* arrived in stereo.
But who was it she had come to see?
Was it her father? brother? lover?"—
He stopped. She was crying, just as planned,
but something had shifted between them
as he finished telling the story:
it had taken on its own green life,
apart from him and his strategies.
"That was great," she said into the dark,
not reaching for him. And he was pleased.

53

n o t h i n g

Once he was back home, driving around doing nothing
with a woman he'd loved decades ago, he'd asked her
to be his girlfriend in tenth grade but she wrote back
saying, No thank you, I've already got a boyfriend:

they were both long-married now, happily, with kids,
they were satisfied in their separate lives, nothing
was going to happen tonight or ever, they were headed
back to her house where their families were waiting

when they passed a convenience mart whose gas pumps
were on fire, colossal pillars of flame blistering
the canopy, not a soul in sight, not a car, nothing:
he pulled to the curb and they sat watching them blaze

waiting for the big explosion, for somebody to come
put the fire out, for something to stop this burning
that might last all night long—but after a minute
he put the car in gear and drove away, saying nothing.

g o o d y e a r

One brittle fall dusk near the end
of The Year of Bitter Words,
he was trying to clear his head by raking the yard hard

when he sensed someone,
or some*thing*, something *big*, moving up behind him, slowly:
as his hackles raised and he turned around
waiting for it to show itself,

a blimp glided directly overhead

and stopped as if it had been summoned there,
a ceiling sealing off his property.
Its lights were out. It issued a profound hum.
He knew it must have come from the afternoon football game
where fans cheered its frozen spiral
and expensive lofty footage of themselves,

but still it felt like an omen, not unexpected,
this streamlined nightmare cloud stuck to his ash trees,
this darker darkness in the sky
eclipsing Venus and all the early stars,
casting a shadow's shadow on his upturned face—

this Goodyear, waiting, headed somewhere else.

w a i t

Her car rumbles into and down the drive,
now I can stop worrying, she's come home,
soon I will hear her climbing the steps
up to the back porch, a rustle of bags,
a prefatory jingle of keys as she counts
to the ones she needs to get inside,
a fumbling for the handle in the dark

and then the locks relax and in she comes,
bringing the night, the cold, her breath
into the house where I have been waiting
for hours for her to lift her lonely hand
and feel for the switch on the kitchen wall:

it is very dark inside the human body
with only the holes in the head for light
and not even that in a still-darkened house.

a f t e r   s o n g

Once she was gone, he never quite forgot
how she would lift up her voice in song after song
from a distant corner of their first house
at any time, for no apparent reason,

her unselfconscious buoyant alto rising
into childhood hymns, show tunes, pop standards,
arias composed of newspaper headlines,
songs without words, it didn't matter,

anything she touched could lead to music
as she cooked or made up the bed or got dressed,
her bittersweet solos filling the rooms
between them with diminishing sound

that would stop if she heard him coming
so he sat dead still, waiting, not humming along,
afraid he might scare away this bird
he once thought he knew so completely,

lifting up her voice in song after song
for reasons that had nothing to do with him.

the angel

unhooks her wings after another long day.
They are her glory but also a burden,
binding her chest and making her sacrum ache.
She reaches behind herself to unfasten
them without the least hesitation or thought,
letting the sweaty wings collapse to the floor.

The angel scratches a ticklish spot
and starts to let down the radiant hair
sometimes mistaken for a halo,
unweaving her braid as gracefully
as she composed its strands long ago.
But how can those backward fingers see?

And then she slips off her slip in the dark.
My heart is tinder to that holy spark.

g l o r y

If a woman have long hair, it is a glory.   I Corinthians 11:15

Every time I use that green shampoo
or pass some unknown woman on the street
who's used it that morning, her hair still wet,
I inhale deeply
                    and think again of you
on top of me, your waterfall of hair
covering my hands covering your breasts
and cascading forward onto my chest
as you leaned down,
                            that charged green air
filling my head as I closed my eyes
and surrendered my skin to the exquisite
whispers of your hair as you swept it
over my drowning face,
                            my fingers rising
entwined in your glory, as they still do
every time you use that green shampoo.

h o n e y s u c k l e

for Marie and Seamus Heaney

Sweetest of weeds, it threads the margins
of early May's illuminated manuscript
with a flourish of flowers that we'll pick
once they deepen to buttery yellow,
pinching the bottoms off and gently pulling
the pistils out until a single drop
of honey gleams at the base of each bloom
and we suckle from that little nipple,
drunk on the updrafts of aromatic air
and nectar blooming on our once-mortal tongues.

five

poem typed on an old machine with a bi-chrome ribbon

All of the descenders
and some of the bottoms
of some of the letters
and one solitary little *a*
in the middle of the page

are red, the mostly black

lines slowly beginning
to catch fire from below,
the temperature climbing
until they are all holy,
uttered by ruddy Jesus.

this page

The letters glitter blackly
in afternoon sunlight,
as if the impact of these words
exposed the anthracite

just under the soft surface,
ready for burning,
the shadow manuscript to which
this world's returning.

b r u i s e s

Bruises linger longer as we age, staking their claim
on the soon-to-be-rotten sweet fruit of our flesh.

•

A baby's blank skin never holds a grudge for long.
It's a time-lapse miracle, putrefaction in reverse.

•

The hickeys I left on her neck were collapsed rainbows,
unfolding their colors backward under her sweater.

•

The edgy world keeps touching us, to prove it does exist:
too much touch and blood blooms just under the skin.

•

I swear I don't remember where I got these blemishes,
these stormclouds in a pale sky, like fabulous animals . . .

•

Death is so heavy-handed. Doesn't anybody want to see
all the marks he keeps leaving on me, in secret places?

•

The last bruise we suffer will deepen and expand
till we're nothing but bruise, camouflaged for darkness.

t w i t c h

Subversive nerves
are staging a *coup d'etat*
in my right eyelid.

They've struck before
in the outlying provinces
of exhausted legs and fingers,
but now they've seized the capital
and I can't stop quivering.
Why doesn't somebody notice me
winking and wincing?

I even twitch in my sleep,
the dream-focus jittery,
quick involuntary flickers of muscle
under my blindfold
just before the fatigued men fire.

My eyelid taps out the morse
of their terms of surrender:
You must admit you are no longer
in control of anything.

p h a n t o u m

Where are the phantom words that got away,
the ones I knew I'd never see again,
the ones I thought would change my life
with a little more luck and a lot more time?

The ones I knew I'd never see again
wait like huge fish just below the surface.
With a little more luck and a lot more time,
they would've fed a grateful multitude.

Wait! Like huge fish just below the surface,
perfect words tease the end of this line:
they would've fed a grateful multitude
but now they're gone, a ghostly cryptogram.

Perfect words tease the end of this line.
If only I'd been more patient, or maybe less!
But now they're gone, a ghostly cryptogram
never to be deciphered in this world.

If only I'd been more patient, or maybe less . . .
Plato thought all reality was phantom,
never to be deciphered in this world.
There's an aching where something used to be.

Plato thought all reality was phantom.
Is he the hunched figure stealing my words?
There's an aching where something used to be,
an amputated phrase, a friend, a father—

is he the hunched figure stealing my words,
the ones I thought would change my life?
An amputated phrase, a friend, a father—
where are the phantom worlds that got away?

several dozen
xeroxes
from a hymnal

At the shadowy edge of every copy
floats a wrinkled creature, long thought extinct,
trying to get out of the picture,
its blunt ventral fin
trailing just below the recto page:

my hand, amputated at the wrist
and xeroxed again and again
in this series of grainy amateur snapshots,
its lines of head and heart and fate
eclipsed every time by this open book

that looks like it's been grafted
to the middle of my left palm,
my dirty fingers changed
into a dazzling tablet, holy with noted words,
that I can lift in greeting or farewell.

workshop poem

1.

Deal your poems to the left,
a comfortable rustle of manuscript
circling the table.

Everyone holds the same hand
though everyone will score it differently.

2.

When you read your poems aloud,

why do you flare your nostrils so fiercely,
or, blushing, stroke your neck,
or tap out such a hyperactive meter
with your hidden foot?

And why do you, and you, and you
read so quickly that you blunt all your words,
as if to apologize for having written them
or having inflicted them on us,

who need to hear your poems aloud?

3.

This class is as much about silence
as words, our pauses
necessary as stanza breaks
or the white space underwriting the page.

4.

Welcome to the scriptorium,

all heads down, all pens busy
illuminating the margins of your poem
with helpful commentary
or at least a few amusing doodles.

In the beginning was the word. . .

Everything here ends in manuscript,
hands dancing over dancing feet.

5.

When we speak, we address your poem,
not you,

reverencing it
or at least the ideal poem it could be.

If our words seem obtuse or superficial,
forgive us,

we're trying,
like you, to say something unsayable.

Listen for the words behind our words.

6.

Laughter is permitted, even encouraged:
the muse of workshops is Thalia,
who knows that every good image is a kind of joke,
a familiar surprise.

As during sex or church,
we shouldn't take ourselves too seriously,
though there's nothing more serious
than love or God or words,
all that passion and theophany and craft

and sheer dumb luck.

7.

This is not a courtroom
and you are not the defendant
and we are not judge and jury, rendering verdicts.

This is not an O.R.
and you are not the patient
though it is time to wheel your poem into Recovery.

This is not a shrink's office
and you are not in group therapy
though our hour is up. How does that make you feel?

8.

Balled-up pieces of paper
will surround your desk like little planets.

Listen to them expand,
the slow crackle
of words trying to flatten the pages
and get back to you, the maker of worlds.

Your patience is the unified field
holding everything together
in this universe of originals and revisions.

9.

In the end, as a poet once said,
it all comes down to this:

Who will teach me to write? The page.

poetry reading in a room hung with bayard wootten photographs from depression-era north and south carolina

The poet reads his measured words to us
and also to Doc Hoppas of Penland,
who grins and lifts his fiddle to his chin,
leaning back in a canebottom chair.
He could set these lines to music.

The poet reads a poem about childhood
to the woman who remembers being a girl
and her girls, who dream of being women.
Their faces yearn toward the distant light
with identical evasive features and vast eyes.

The poet reads a poem about art
and Ben Owen listens, big head down,
big hands glazed with water and light,
pulling up spinning clay on the wheel.
Somebody will use this pot he's making.

The poet reads a poem about food
but the hungry fisherman mending nets
never lifts his head, his face hat-shadowed,
his fingers shining like minnows in the sun.
The heavy weave has put both feet to sleep.

The poet reads a poem about work
and the family of four tobacco farmers
pauses among the thick chest-high leaves.
They share cool water from a mason jar,
their sticky hands clear through the glass.

The poet reads a poem about race
to the black woman with an empty plate,
a cat sniffing her patched skirt and apron.
She stares straight ahead, not even trying
to hide the holes in her safety-pinned sweater.

The poet reads a poem about fate
but the three spinster sisters in solid black
keep carding and spinning: they never stop
for anyone or anything at any time.
Their wheel in silhouette is a dark blur.

The poet reads a poem about poetry
to Zack McHone and his stack of books.
His shirt is dirty, his bootsoles are worn,
his hands are rough from a lifetime of work,
but they're clean as the precious pages

of the open volume shining on his lap,
and he may be old and alone, but he can still
hold a book and read it by the firelight
as well as anybody gathered in this room,
the bright language filling his head and ours

as the poet finishes reading his measured words.

six

those words

for Shirley Anders and Scott Byrd

I never could arrange it in this life
but I like to imagine you meeting at last
in the vast Library of the World to Come
where (as certain faithful scholars said)
all the truly good books ever written
are made available to the righteous dead—

probably in Fiction, one of you laughing
at a novel some angel somehow judged worthy
and reading aloud its ludicrous passages
in such a sweet accent, with such mirth,
that the other approaches and joins in
with so much gusto you're asked to leave

and so you do, eager to start gossiping
about which books are mutual favorites
and what to admit to your Everlasting Stacks,
the poetry and stories and bedtime trash
you recall with sudden utter clarity
down to the page, the line, the syllable:

this is paradise, this conversation,
each word improving the articulate light
just as it used to when we'd sit and visit
or you'd write a pithy card or note or letter.
Look how I saved them all, in labelled boxes!
Look how those words can still fill up my hands.

four-leaf clover

In all my unlucky life, I never found one
until now, pressed between unabridged pages
in an old Webster's International Dictionary,
floating among an illustration of clouds
like a colossal kite pulling away from earth.

Maybe some hopeful young woman plucked this
in a field among cattle over half a century ago
and ran it, bright green and sweet and wet,
to the house whose only other book was the Bible
and hid it over the definition of itself:

she'd sneak back nightly and touch it for luck,
believing this was the devoutly longed-for sign
that her fiancé would soon be home from the war
and they'd get married and work the family farm,
living in clover the rest of their life together,

not knowing it would fade over the decades
until it was the same drab greenish-brown
as the uniform he wore in her bedside picture,
the little hearts of its leaflets flattened and brittle,
these columns of dense black words its only honey.

to my father
on the anniversary
of his death

What a grizzly day, gray and drizzly,
sky the same drained uncolor as your deathbed face,

today's light stuck on the other side
of a dense cloud dome baffling the March-third sun:

I fill clear glass vases with daffodils
cut while wandering the yard and neighborhood,

their stems green blurs inside my hands,
their petals like flimsy flames barely lighting the way

as I look for you, or the memory of you,
anywhere in the deep late winter of this underworld.

the whistler

At first I think it's in my head,
this unearthly melody I can't identify,
but then I realize, no,
it's all around me, notes filling the quad
like drops of water will fill a basin
to the top and beyond.

I look around me for the source
and finally see a tiny man
standing on the steep steps of Main Hall,
arms folded behind him, head back, whistling
with astonishing volume
a fluid tune I still don't recognize.

He seems to be Chinese:
maybe he's homesick and this song
takes him back to that night by the river,
her hair in the moonlight
flowing over his hands like a black current . . .
Or maybe it helps him forget.

Or maybe he's just making it up
as he goes along, a breathless improvisation
here in the American twilight
that has nothing to do with anything
but itself, notes following notes,
their round sounds flowing off the bricks.

He stands still but sways
forward and backward and sideways,
a rapt broadcasting through light drizzle
to no one but me
I find when I look around for another person,
to prove this isn't a dream.

But so what if it is?
It's a good long one and I needed a song
as much as he needed to pour one out,
this migratory warbler
still whistling as I walk away,
raindrops kissing my skin like quarter notes.

ella fitzgerald

When her voice sweetens the speakers in the store,
suddenly my legs begin to ache
for the six decades she stood and sung and swung,
coaxing the innocent naughtiness
out of Gershwin and Porter and the popular songbook,
every lyrical twist enunciated
crisply, playfully, even the wildest scat articulated
as if it should make perfect sense,
which it did, somehow, to her body and all its parts,
she ba ba shoo do-do-do boing boing,
fingers snapping, head swiveling slightly, deep mouth
with its pearly teeth shaping
the song as it rose from sugary depths, feet tapping
at the end of her too too solid

legs, those legs eventually amputated, lost to diabetes,
as utterly vanished as the words
to "Mack the Knife" live in concert in Berlin, 1960,
but Ella doesn't give up or panic
or miss a beat with her improvisations, *what's the next*
verse to this song now, a-a-a-ah,
somethin' 'bout cash, where the heck is she going, how
will she get herself and her Fellas
and the listeners then and later out of this, the most
inventive instrument is the human
voice in flight, the phantom text never quite resurfaces
but the tune doesn't falter once
on her tongue, the Germans jump to their feet cheering,
they're devouring her with applause.

the family laugh

for Miriam Marty Clark

On my way from the kitchen to the living room,
I heard you laugh while cooking and your mother
laugh while telling a story to the dinner guests

and it was uncanny, precisely the same sound,
an identical inarticulate explosion of delight
at some absurd turn in the recipe or narrative.

I stood frozen between your matching happiness
just like the time I heard my cousin's cackle—
its gentle unforced tone, its melodious cheer—

and shivered because it was just like Messalina,
my favorite fun-loving aunt, dead for many years
yet alive in the genuine mirth of her daughter.

What better legacy to leave my son than this?—
the family laugh, a manner of taking pleasure,
an antidote to poisonous genetics or habits,

the lethal words and looks and offhand guilt
I've given him without thinking; so that, one day,
somebody might hear him and his son laughing

in exactly the same way, at exactly the same time,
and hear a perfect echo of me and my parents
and all the unlikely generations of laughter

back up the Appalachians, across the dour ocean
to a place where joy was as precious as food,
all the way back to the original couple who saw

something in the garden that made them feel odd,
that inspired a sweet illogical noise, the first laugh.
It baffled the animals, but God saw that it was good.

about the author

Michael McFee has published five collections of poetry: *Colander* (Carnegie Mellon University Press, 1996), *To See* (a collaboration with photographer Elizabeth Matheson: North Carolina Wesleyan College Press, 1991), *Sad Girl Sitting on a Running Board* (Gnomon Press, 1991), *Vanishing Acts* (Gnomon, 1989), and *Plain Air* (University Presses of Florida, 1983). He has also edited the poetry anthology *The Language They Speak Is Things to Eat: Poems by Fifteen Contemporary North Carolina Poets* (University of North Carolina Press, 1994) and the fiction anthology *This Is Where We Live: Short Stories by 25 Contemporary North Carolina Writers* (UNC Press, 2000). He teaches poetry-writing and literature at UNC-Chapel Hill.